help **me**
UNDERSTAND™

Feeling *Anger* &
Learning *Delight*™

REAL

mvpk

Lucas Tames the Anger Dragon™

SOPHIA DAY®

Written by Megan Johnson   Illustrated by Stephanie Strouse

WELCOME to the WORLD OF

mvpkids

Everything we create is with the intention of nurturing
a child's character. Our mission is to equip parents, teachers and
caregivers to engage with kids through inspiring entertainment.

nurture
LITERACY™

cultivate
MENTORSHIP™

inspire
CHARACTER®

expand
EDUCATION™

enrich
ENTERTAINMENT™

help**me**
UNDERSTAND™

Feeling *Anger* &
Learning *Delight*™

REAL

mvpkids®

Lucas
Tames
the
Anger
Dragon™

SOPHIA DAY®

Written by Megan Johnson   Illustrated by Stephanie Strouse

The Sophia Day® Creative Team-
Stephanie Strouse, Megan Johnson,
Kayla Pearson, Timothy Zowada, Carol Sauder, Mel Sauder

A **special thank you** to our team of reviewers who graciously
give us feedback, edits and help ensure that our products
remain accurate, applicable and genuinely diverse.

Published and Distributed by MVP Kids Media, LLC -
Mesa, Arizona, USA
Printed by RR Donnelley Asia Printing Solutions, Ltd -
Dongguan City, Guangdong Province, China

Designed by Stephanie Strouse

ISBN 978-164370758-7
DOM May 2019
Job # 12-001-01

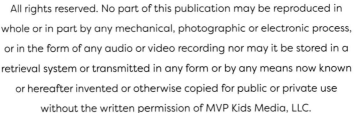

*May your childhood be filled with
adventure, your days with hope
and your learnings with wisdom,
and may you continuously grow as
an MVP Kid, preparing to lead a
responsible, meaningful life.*

-SOPHIA DAY

Lucas woke up full of energy.

"WAKE UP!
WAKE UP!"

he said to his brother.

LeBron pulled
the covers over
his head and
groaned.

Lucas
sulked
away.

"Maybe mom will
play cars with me,"
he thought.

But when Lucas found
Mom in the kitchen, she
was feeding breakfast
to his sister, Jada, while
bouncing a baby on her hip.

"Mom won't have time
for me," he thought.

"Hey, Dad! Can you...?"

"Good morning, bud.
It's your day to feed the dogs."

Lucas dropped his car.
He *slammed* the
back door, scooped up the
dog food and just as he was
pouring the food...

...Rocky *CRASHED* into him with a big wet kiss!

The dog food went flying...

The scoop went flying...

LUCAS WENT FLYING!

ROCKY

Lucas felt like a

DRAGON
POPPED UP

from inside of him
as he stood back up.

The dragon kicked the scoop.
He yelled at Rocky.
The dragon stomped his feet and breathed out fire!

Then the dragon
went inside and
stomped
up the stairs to
his bedroom.

"I'M SO ANGRY!"

Lucas yelled.

His brother, now
awake, slid quickly
under his sheets, off
the mattress and hid
underneath his bed.

Mom knocked on the door and looked in.

Surprised to see a dragon instead of her sweet little boy, she said in her bravest voice,

"Who are you, **great dragon,** and what have you done with my boy?"

Lucas was afraid that his mom wouldn't love him as an angry dragon. He didn't want her to know he was scared so he breathed out a big puff of smoke.

"Oh, I'm not **scared away** by a little smoke and fire," Mom said, bravely meeting eyes with the dragon. "I hear that you are angry, but you may not throw things, no matter how angry you are."

Mom reached for
Lucas to hold him
and keep him
safe until he
calmed down.

"Today *stinks*."

Lucas kept his voice big and gruff so he wouldn't feel so small.

"Your anger is controlling you right now, stomping around and breathing fire like a dragon..."

"Lucky for you,
I know how to tame a dragon!
Let's take some deep breaths. A dragon only
breathes fire with short, huffy breaths."

"But a dragon **can't breathe fire** with BIG, deep, *slow* breaths."

Mom reached for Lucas' hand and placed it on her shoulder.

"You feel my breathing and copy me, OK? Here we go."

Mom and Lucas took BIG, deep, *slow* breaths together until Lucas had calmed down.

A few dragon scales tumbled to the floor
and his nostrils stopped smoking.

"Why are you having such a hard day?" Mom asked.

"LeBron wouldn't play with me, you don't have time for me and the dog food is a mess! Today *stinks*."

"And I
hurt my elbow."

"That reminds me.
I brought you a bandage."

As his mom
comforted him,
the dragon
started to cry.

His tough, scaly
armor began to
fall away.

Tear by tear, scale by scale, the dragon dissolved until...

...all that was left was **the boy, Lucas.**

"Mom, am I *bad*?"

Lucas was concerned.

"No, dear. I love you all the time. Everyone gets angry sometimes.

You just need to learn to
tame that anger dragon
so you don't hurt people
or destroy things when you
feel angry."

"It *scares* me when

I act like
a dragon.

When it starts, I don't
know how to stop."

"Sometimes our anger is so **BIG** because we're *hiding* a lot of other feelings behind it.

You were sad
that LeBron wouldn't
play with you.

You were scared
that I wouldn't have
time for you.

You were **annoyed** because you would have to clean up the dog food.

And you were **physically hurt** when Rocky knocked you over.

Is that right?"

"And Dad ignored me." Lucas added.

"Sad, scared, annoyed, hurt and ignored don't feel very powerful, so you hid them with anger. It's hard to have such big feelings. Acting like a dragon makes you feel bigger, but it doesn't solve your problems. You need to tell me how you're feeling before it gets out of hand like this."

Mom could hear Jada fussing and the baby crying downstairs.

"Tell you what," said Mom, "I need to go downstairs to take care of Jada and the baby."

"Let's pretend you're starting the day again. Get back in bed, pretend to wake up and try to see today as a happy day. Instead of starting the day angry that things aren't going your way, **RESET** your attitude and **try to find** *delight*."

"What is delight?"

Lucas wondered.

Mom explained, "Delight is happiness, or joy. You can use delight to help shield you from the anger dragon. The world is full of wonderful people and things. If you look for the joy, you'll find it hard to be angry. This really is a beautiful day, not a stinky one. Try to find the good."

"Okay, LeBron, back in bed!

Time for a
RESET!"

announced Lucas.

Both boys climbed back in bed and pretended to be sleeping.

Lucas got up and went over to Lebron's bed.

"WAKE UP! WAKE UP!"

he said to his brother.

"Just five more minutes," giggled LeBron.

"Hey Mom! Can you play cars with me?"

Lucas asked hopefully.

"I'd really like to play cars with you when I have everyone dressed and fed," said Mom as she prepared a bottle for the foster* baby.

*A foster child is a child who needs to live with a new, safe family for a while.

Sometimes it was difficult
to have little kids and babies around,
but for the most part, Lucas liked that
his family kept babies who needed a
little extra help for a while.

After all, that's how LeBron and Jada
became his brother and sister!

Lucas smiled. "They're cute and
fun as long as I don't have
to change diapers."

Lucas turned, expecting to see Dad in the kitchen. His place was set at the table. It wasn't his favorite breakfast, but there was fresh orange juice.

"I guess it's not all bad," he thought.

He saw Dad outside sweeping up the dog food and went out to join him.

Dad handed him the dustpan.

"I'm sorry I ignored you, Lucas," said Dad. "It's a beautiful day. I was thinking you boys and I could build a raceway for the cars out here after breakfast."

"That sounds great, Dad!"

"Mom told me to look for joys today," said Lucas. "And I guess that the dog food spilling gave you and me a little bit of time alone, even if it is cleaning up together. That makes me happy."

"Now that's a great attitude, son! I love to have special time with you, no matter what we're doing. Now, let's see if we can all build a ramp for that raceway!"

When your anger's like a dragon
And there's fire in your roar
Take deep breaths: in one and two,
Then breathe out, three and four.

Peel away the dragon's scales
And find out what's beneath.
You may find you're feeling
Scared or lonely underneath.

You might think that breathing fire
And being ferocious makes you strong
But hurting others, throwing things
And yelling words is wrong.

Instead of being angry
About what isn't going your way,
Look for something good
You can enjoy about today.

No matter what the day may bring
Make your attitude right.
Look for something wonderful
And choose to seek delight.

LEARN & DISCUSS

Lucas is learning to understand his angry feelings and how to handle them well. Learn with Lucas and discuss how you can tame your anger dragon, too!

When I was angry, I did things to make myself feel bigger and more powerful. I yelled, kicked things, threw things and slammed my door. Mom helped me remember that hurting things or people and yelling are not okay. They do not really help me feel better.

What do you do when you are angry?

Why are these destructive or hurtful things not helpful for solving the situation or problems?

Knowing how your body feels when you are angry can help you control your feelings before they become too big. When I'm angry, I feel hot inside my chest and I want to yell. I don't feel in control.

Describe what you feel like when you're angry.

How does your head feel? How does your chest feel?

What kind of facial expressions do you make?

Mom helped me take deep breaths to calm down before we talked about my anger. Deep breathing is one great way to calm yourself. Other tools are exercise, going outside or stretching.

What tools do you like to use to calm down when you are frustrated, angry or scared?

Practice taking deep breaths now so that it will be easier when you are upset.

I began to gain control of myself again when mom helped me to see that there were a lot of reasons I was upset. I had a lot of feelings I was hiding and I needed to feel understood. When I identified my hurts, my anger became more manageable.

Think about the last time you were angry. Were there other feelings you were hiding, too?

Does talking with someone about your feelings help you feel less angry?

I learned that being angry isn't bad. Every feeling has a purpose. Anger helps us identify when someone is treated unjustly or a situation is wrong or unfair. Often, however, we feel angry when our expectations aren't met or we don't get our way. Remember that anger itself isn't wrong, but don't do something wrong out of anger.

When have you been angry for good reasons?

When have you been angry for selfish reasons?

Have you done anything in anger that you regret?

LeBron and I reset the day by pretending to start again. Re-playing the events that caused my anger and choosing to see it in a different way helped me change my mood. I learned to look for the good in things.

Next time you're feeling angry, look for good things around you or name things that make you feel happy or thankful.

Does this help you manage your anger better?

How can you help your child tame the anger dragon?

Understand the Anger Brain. When a child is agitated, the brain enters a self-preservation reflex of fight, flight or freeze. In this state the brain is not capable of rationalizing or learning. In addition, your child may not be fully in control of his physical responses. A caregiver must first use techniques to soothe and calm the child before attempting to talk through the situation.

It is likely that your child didn't go from relaxed and happy to angry as quickly as it seems. Frustration builds over time and reaches a tipping point or explosion. Help your child develop an awareness of "triggers" so that he can resolve feelings on a more manageable scale, before an outburst occurs.

Meet Hidden Needs. When your child is angry, first calm yourself and prepare to address your child's needs. Although anger might appear to be a direct response to an event, it is often a result of many underlying needs, such as hunger, fatigue or sadness, and was only triggered by the immediate issue at hand. Try to identify the hidden needs and respond to the needs rather than reacting to the emotions.

Lower your stance and get eye level with your child. Kids frequently struggle with feeling small and powerless. Anger is often used to make a child feel more powerful. Kneeling to your child's eye level will decrease the need for an angry defense.

Practice Calming Techniques. New brain pathways are best developed in a calm state. Practice these calming techniques when you and your child are both feeling calm, and they will be more easily accessed during times of heightened emotions.

Deep breaths increase the amount of oxygen to your brain, stimulating part of the nervous system that promotes calmness and reduces physical anger responses. Lead your child through taking several deep breaths. It may be helpful to place your child's hand on your shoulder, chest or stomach to feel how long and deep the breaths should be. Older children can try a "take five" strategy. Spread the fingers of one hand and trace around them with the other pointer finger. Take in deep breaths while tracing up a finger and breathe out while tracing downward.

Other calming techniques include stretching exercises, constructive physical activity or changing environments such as going outside. Sometimes having a focus phrase to repeat can be calming, too. Older kids may be able to memorize the poem at the end of this story to recite as a calming tool.

Celebrate successful de-escalations. Rebuild connection with your child, and make sure physical needs for food and water are met. Try sitting in a pillow fort or having a picnic snack. Wrap a blanket around you and your child to promote a sense of security and love. When a child feels calm, secure and cared for following an episode of intense emotion, trust with supportive adults will be established. Then, your child will be confident in being heard without making a scene the next time.

Meet the

featured in
Lucas Tames the Anger Dragon™

LUCAS MILLER

LeBRON MILLER

Also featuring...

MR. JAMES MILLER
"Dad"

MRS. ELIZABETH MILLER
"Mom"

MILLIE
Foster Child

JADA MILLER
Sister

ROCKY
Family Dog

Grow up with our mvpkids

CELEBRATE!™
Board Books
Ages 0-6

Our **CELEBRATE**™ board books for toddlers and preschoolers focus on social, emotional, educational and physical needs. Helpful Teaching Tips are included in each book to equip parents to guide their children deeper into the subject of each book.

Celebrate!™
Paperbacks
Ages 4-8

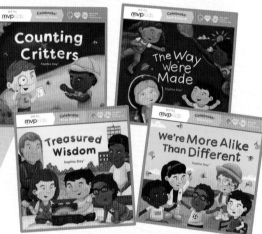

Our **Celebrate!**™ paperback books for Pre-K to Grade 2 focus on social, emotional, educational and physical needs. Helpful Teaching Tips are included in each book to equip mentors and parents. Also available are expertly written curriculum and interactive e-book apps.

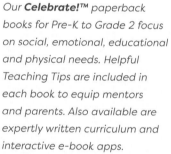

helpme™
BECOME
Early Elementary
Ages 4-10

Our **Help Me Become**™ series for early elementary readers tells three short stories in each book of our MVP Kids® inspiring character growth. Each story concludes with a discussion guide to help the child process the story and apply the concepts.

help me UNDERSTAND™
Elementary
Ages 6-12

Help your children grow in understanding emotions by collecting the entire **Help Me Understand**™ series!

*Our **Help Me Understand**™ series for elementary readers shares the stories of our MVP Kids® learning to understand and manage specific emotions. Readers will gain tools to take responsibility for their own emotions and develop healthy relationships.*

www.mvpkids.com

YONG CHEN

LEO RUSSO

FRANKIE RUSSO

JULIA ROJAS

GABBY GONZALEZ

ANNIE JAMES

AANYA PATEL

BLAKE JAMES

SARAH COHEN-GOLDSTEIN

LeBRON MILLER

LUCAS MILLER

FAITH JORDAN

MIRIAM NASSER

EZEKIEL JORDAN

OLIVIA WAGNER

LIAM JOHNSON

Get to know our MVP Kids®!

You will learn and grow with them from book to book. Each MVP Kid® has a personal back story and unique personality, making it easier for kids of all kinds to see themselves and their friends within our books!

www.mvpkids.com

Real MVP Kids

@realMVPkids